This Notebook Belongs To

___